SPORTS FOR SPROUTS

KARATE

Holly Karapetkova

ROURKE PUBLISHING

Vero Beach, Florida 32964

www.rourkepublishing.com

Photo credits: Cover © Gerville Hall; Title Page © Wendy Nero, Crystal Kirk, Leah-Anne Thompson, vnosokin, Gerville Hall, Rob Marmion; Page 3 © Gerville Hall; Page 4 © Gerville Hall; Page 7 © Gerville Hall; Page 8 © Gerville Hall; Page 11 © Gerville Hall; Page 12 © Gerville Hall; Page 14 © Gerville Hall; Page 17 © Jason Lugo; Page 18 © Gerville Hall; Page 21 © Gerville Hall; Page 22 © Gerville Hall, Jason Lugo; Page 23 © Gerville Hall

Editor: Meg Greve

Cover and page design by Nicola Stratford, Blue Door Publishing

Library of Congress Cataloging-in-Publication Data

Karapetkova, Holly.
  Karate / Holly Karapetkova.
    p. cm. -- (Sports for sprouts)
  ISBN 978-1-60694-324-3 (hard cover)
  ISBN 978-1-60694-824-8 (soft cover)
  ISBN 978-1-60694-565-0 (bilingual)
  1. Karate--Juvenile literature. I. Title.
  GV1114.3.K35 2010
  796.815'3--dc22
                                        2009002257

Rourke Publishing
Printed in the United States of America, North Mankato, Minnesota
072710
072610LP-B

ROURKE PUBLISHING

www.rourkepublishing.com - rourke@rourkepublishing.com
Post Office Box 643328 Vero Beach, Florida 32964

2

I like
karate.

3

I wear a white or black uniform called a **gi**.

I wear a colored belt.
The belt tells my **rank**.

7

My karate class starts with a bow.

We learn **stances**. We learn punches.

We learn how to block and kick.

We learn **katas**. Katas have punches, blocks, and kicks.

We do katas again and again to learn the motions.

We listen to our sensei.

19

We are always safe and careful not to hurt each other.

Glossary

gi (GEE): A gi, or do-gi, is the outfit worn in karate. The gi includes a jacket and pants and is tied with a belt.

karate (kah-RAH-tee): Karate means empty hand in Japanese because karate athletes fight without weapons. They use kicks and punches to fight and defend themselves.

katas (KAH-tahz): Katas are series of punches, kicks, and blocks done in a certain order. Karate students practice katas many times in order to learn basic motions.

rank (RANGK): In karate, a person's rank tells how skillful he or she is. The rank is measured by the color of the belt.

sensei (SEN-say): Sensei is the Japanese word for teacher. Karate students call their teacher sensei.

stances (STANSS-iz): Stances are starting positions that prepare the body for action.

Index

Websites

www.akakarate.com
www.ska.org
www.usankf.org

About The Author

Holly Karapetkova, Ph.D., loves writing books and poems for kids and adults. She teaches at Marymount University and lives in the Washington, D.C., area with her husband, her son K.J., and her two dogs, Muffy and Attila.